Also by Laurel Geise

The Book of Life:
Universal Truths for a New Millennium

The New Laws of Spirit

Prophetic Leadership: A Call to Action

The Jesus Seeds

Igniting Your Soul-Guided Life

LAUREL GEISE

BALBOA.
PRESS

A DIVISION OF HAY HOUSE

Balboa Press books may be ordered through booksellers or by contacting:

Balboa Press
A Division of Hay House
1663 Liberty Drive
Bloomington, IN 47403
www.balboapress.com
1-(877) 407-4847

Because of the dynamic nature of the Internet, any web addresses or links contained in this book may have changed since publication and may no longer be valid. The views expressed in this work are solely those of the author and do not necessarily reflect the views of the publisher, and the publisher hereby disclaims any responsibility for them.

The author of this book does not dispense medical advice or prescribe the use of any technique as a form of treatment for physical, emotional, or medical problems without the advice of a physician, either directly or indirectly. The intent of the author is only to offer information of a general nature to help you in your quest for emotional and spiritual well-being. In the event you use any of the information in this book for yourself, which is your constitutional right, the author and the publisher assume no responsibility for your actions.

Any people depicted in stock imagery provided by Thinkstock are models, and such images are being used for illustrative purposes only.
Certain stock imagery © Thinkstock.

ISBN: 978-1-4525-7253-6 (sc)
ISBN: 978-1-4525-7255-0 (hc)
ISBN: 978-1-4525-7254-3 (e)

Library of Congress Control Number: 2013906935

Printed in the United States of America.

Balboa Press rev. date: 04/29/2013

For those who courageously
step forth into the magnificence
of an authentic soul guided life:

May you be showered with God's grace,
kissed by the Holy Spirit, and
embraced by the love
that is Christ consciousness.

Table of Contents

Preface ix

Part I

Introduction 3
The Seeds 9
The Creation 11
Recognizing the Divine Within 15
The Quest 19
Bringing the Vibration Home 21
The Vibratory Scale 25
A New Reality 29
Seeing the World through God's Eyes 31
The Greater Now 35
The Calling 37

Part II

The Next Chapter 41
Hieroglyphics 45
Connecting with the Soul 49
Vibrational Density 53
The Continuum of Change 57
Seeing a New Future 59
Our Home, Our Kingdom 61

Living in the Kingdom...65

The Bridge 67

Higher Senses 71

The Continuation of the Christ Consciousness.................75

The Hum of God's Love..77

The Authentic One 81

Part III

Our New Life 87

A Collective Blink..91

The Bridge Builders..93

The Leap 97

Are You Ready?..101

What Are the Signs?..103

Walk in His Steps...107

Appendix: Soul Journaling.......................................113

In Gratitude and Appreciation.................................117

About the Author..119

Preface

My first glimpse into what would become *The Jesus Seeds* began innocently during an evening meditation as I relaxed in my favorite easy chair. After a long day at work as a business executive, my evening meditation provided a sacred balance to the demands of excessive office hours and off-the-charts stress levels. This was my nightly practice to bring me back to myself.

I relaxed into silence and found my awareness suddenly transported to another time and place. I was standing in front of a large pool of water that was so calm and clear that the early dawn light bounced from the reflective surface to the barren mountains in the distance. It was desert dry, and the air was crisp. I was in Qumran many thousands of years ago; I was an Essene. As I prepared for my morning prayers with a cleansing ritual, I extended my hands toward the water. In a split second, I was back in my easy chair, and I opened my eyes. This brief glimpse into another time stretched me beyond my analytical mind. It propelled me to find out everything that I could about the Essenes, which I now know were a Jewish religious sect known for their austere practices and deep devotion to God. This intimate experience of a time two thousand years ago, although as real as the hand in front of my face, began to fade into memory. As was my practice, I dutifully recorded it in my soul journal and went on with life.

Now, fast forward eight years later. I am in Israel, on a group tour and engulfed in the magic of this historic land. Each day brought with it experiences to walk in the steps of Jesus Christ and to look upon the world through his eyes. We spent time in Jerusalem as well as in a kibbutz on the shores of the Sea of Galilee. We stopped at the River Jordan and were baptized in the cool water. We continued on to the Dead Sea and floated with effortless ease in the densely rich mineral waters. We planned a stop at Qumran to see the archeological ruins and to walk the mountains where Christ had walked.

Our group awakened before dawn and boarded the tour bus for a short ride to Qumran. We arrived at the site before the gates were open; we had been granted special permission to enter the ancient compound and walk up the mountain. As we climbed, the sun rose slowly over the desert. People began seeking caves where Jesus may have prayed and meditated.

In my wanderings, I separated from the group and explored the archaeological ruins. I walked along the dusty pathways and crumbling rocks that were once homes, libraries, and temples. Completely alone, I turned a corner and stopped in awe as I saw a familiar outline of a mountain in the distance. My eyes dropped, and I realized I was standing in front of an ancient ritual bathing pool. Although it was empty, the familiarity triggered an energy that descended into my body and shook me so intensely that I fell to my knees. I lifted my head and realized that I was gazing upon the ritual bathing pool that I had experienced in my meditation over eight long years ago.

With my head reeling and my body shaking, I received a deafening acknowledgment from inside my being. I was an Essene two thousand years ago, I had lived in Qumran, and Jesus had been a friend. I thought of him as a brother and had received many teachings from him that were planted deep within my soul. The seeds would incubate until a future time when the world would be ready to accept the guidance that would facilitate our next evolutionary steps.

This experience was my initiation into a journey that would culminate in *The Jesus Seeds*. Stunned by this experience, I devoutly recorded it in my soul journal but did not speak of it to anyone. I was afraid that I would be ridiculed for having a "Jesus experience" in the Holy Land.

Many years passed, and from time to time I would receive a message during my morning soul journaling (see the appendix) confirming that I would write a book called *The Jesus Seeds*. And yet as time passed, I grew impatient. This felt like one giant cosmic joke where even the heavens were making fun of my Holy Land experience.

And then it happened. On January 2, 2012, I began to receive a divine transmission that started with the words, "The Jesus Seeds." Over and over like a skipping record in my head, all that I could hear was this phrase. I grabbed a blank journal, put pen to paper, and began to write down what I was hearing. Each Sunday morning for many months to come, I would sit quietly in the silence of my home and be open to write down the words. Without fail, the sentences, paragraphs, and chapters flowed with purpose, grace, and ease. This process continued until Sunday morning, April 8, when the last words were written. I put my pen down. It was Easter morning 2012.

I knew with every fiber of my being, and the certainty of my soul, that I needed to share what had been given to me. There was only one problem. Although I had full faith in the next steps that I had to take, I was afraid that I would be ostracized for the ideas and concepts in this book. I have a master's degree in business administration and worked in the financial services sector for thirty years. None of this made any sense to my rational mind, and it certainly did not fit neatly into the life I was living. The urgency of my soul overpowered the fear of my mind, and I now share *The Jesus Seeds* with you.

Congratulations on following your intuition. By simply picking up this book, you have taken a step to lift and shift your consciousness. The words in this book will create a vibrational expansion within your awareness. As an evolutionary primer, it is not important to intellectualize what you are reading, but rather to feel the energy of what is being communicated in your heart, body, and soul. As you read, you may feel lightheaded, fall asleep, or feel tingles of remembrance moving through your body. Whatever your experience, continue to read and absorb the energy of the message. The precepts shared are not meant to change or replace any practice or belief system that you have, but rather to deepen your experience as you awaken to the potential that resides in you. It is a work that has been two thousand years in the making, and it is offered in the hope that it will be received with an open mind and a compassionate heart.

May you be inspired by these words and embrace the future that we will share together.

Laurel Geise

PART I

———⌦———

The Kingdom is within you

and it is outside of you.

—Jesus Christ

Introduction

Ancient cultures knew the secret of human evolution, so much so that many were able to lift their consciousness to move to various dimensions of existence. The binary view of life or death must be vanquished in favor of a new worldview consisting of multidimensional awareness. It may seem like science fiction, but many scientists agree that multiple dimensions exist. If this is true, then why wouldn't we want to explore these dimensions? Granted, we would need to leave the comfort of our three-dimensional existence to explore a multidimensional world, but who says the new world is not even better than our current world? What if a multidimensional existence is ten times or one hundred times more exciting, fulfilling, and loving than our current state? What if miracles were as commonplace and as simple as breathing? What if all of our DNA was suddenly switched on, leading to a higher level of existence seldom ever dreamed of by modern man?

It is these questions and more that we will explore in *The Jesus Seeds*, a contextual rewriting of the future of all mankind. The emergence of Christ consciousness makes all things possible. Jesus taught that we can do what he did and even more.[1] Now is the time to understand what *more* we can do and then put that *more* into action.

Centuries upon centuries have passed since Christ incarnated on our planet. And yet, this being of God-awareness has influenced and continues to influence us every day. We believe we understand his teachings and examples of how to live, but what if there is more to the story? What if we are ready to move to a level of awareness where miracles are our daily birthright? What if hidden in our DNA and our brains are the secrets to embracing our miracle selves? Can you imagine living every moment as a miracle? Einstein said, "There are two ways to see the world. One is as if everything is a miracle. The other view is that there are no miracles."[2] Given this pivotal insight, we are ready to live a life of miracles—a miracle life, if you will.

Seeing the miraculous in every moment is living in a multidimensional existence. The old laws of nature do not apply in this new awareness. The limitations of thought are dissolved; you begin to see the potential of *unlimited* creativity. Taking clues from Einstein's reality and seeking deeper meaning from Jesus and his legacy combine to give us the insight and road map to expanding our existence. This quest will require courage because what we find will reshape our reality. As Jesus

---

[1] John 14:12. (AV)

[2] Albert Einstein Site Online, http://www.alberteinsteinsite.com, Jan. 18, 2012.

explained in the gospel of Thomas, your seeking will bring you to understanding, and then you will be *disturbed*, and then *overwhelmed* by what is and what can be.[3]

Moving forward means we will leave behind our preconceived notions of who we are and step into a newer, bolder experience of who we can be. We will learn, then be disturbed, and finally rejoice in the flourishing of his grace on earth. A new terminology will be required to navigate these nascent waters. As the door opens and we peek through this new portal, giving expression to what we see and feel will go beyond the words of today. Therefore we shall work together to build a new construct for communicating, a new dictionary to define our miraculous expansion.

Looking ahead into unknown territory, every hero knows inherently the journey before him will bring challenges, but also growth. The hero's journey awaits us all. Sri Ramakrishna, an Indian avatar, equates our search for the Divine to that of a man whose hair is on fire desperately seeks a pond. Being on fire brings a compelling urgency to the search. Our commitment to the next steps in our evolution must be fraught with urgency to understand what is possible. Turning over every stone, we will find the Divine. In the gospel of Thomas, Jesus said, "Turn over a rock and I am there. Split a piece of wood, and I am there."[4] In our quest, we shall continuously turn over every stone that is an obstacle to our growth. We will split ourselves open to find the divine flame within us, radiating his grace to all around us.

---

[3] Steven Davies, *The Gospel of Thomas*, (Vermont, Skylight Paths, 2002), p. 3.

[4] Davies, *The Gospel of Thomas*, p. 99.

As adventurers, we must make the commitment to our personal journeys of evolution. No one can take the steps for us, and no one can lead us to where we need to go. Only our souls can light the path for us. As we embark on this quest, we cannot compare our paths to any other path. Each journey to the Divine is as unique as each soul. What we can share is the message of our journeys with others. We can share what we are learning, what we are experiencing, and how our growth is changing our lives.

There will be fear as we move forward. Fear of the unknown is a healthy response. Not knowing what the next steps may bring raises our adrenaline level, and our bodies begin to quake. We will use this body quake to shake loose the roots of our fears and release them so that we can move to a new quake-free zone of being open to the unknown. Anxiety will arise when concepts and experiences that we cannot currently comprehend come face to face with us. Use the energy of the fear and anxiety to move forward; breathe deeply into this energy. Be the catalytic converter to change it from fear to intense curiosity. "What does this new idea mean in my life? How does this experience propel me to a higher level of my greatness? Is there a way that I can share my new understanding to help others with their journey?" We are here on this earth at this time to serve our individual evolution as well as the collective transformation. Each one of us has untold experiences that will be shared to help not only ourselves but others as well. We live in a time of unprecedented change. The harmonics of the earth combine with the frequencies of heaven opening within us a gateway of pure potential. We shall walk hand in hand, sharing our individual strengths with all people as we evolve together in collective wonder.

In evolutionary times, we are called to participate. Great saints and sages throughout the ages knew the commitment required to evolve the human soul; they also knew what was possible. Sri Aurobindo, an Indian philosopher and yogi, spoke of the divinization of the human being—the ability of the human to become Divine. Saint Francis of Assisi prayed to be an instrument of the Divine—being divine peace, love, and compassion while in a human body. The coming together of the human and the Divine is our destiny, our birthright, and our calling. Our souls are crying out for the flame of divine presence as the Christed energy pulsates to ignite the fire in each soul.

Fanning the flames of our divine light will be the key to our evolution. As the flames intensify, our souls will lift up to his divine grace and genuflect in the glory of his love. Divinization of our lives and our planet has begun. Let us collectively explore the next steps of our evolution and be amazed at where the journey goes.

The Seeds

At the core of every soul lie the seeds of truth and grace, waiting for the right frequency of light to awaken them, and then they burst open. It is the bursting of the seeds that brings forth his wisdom into the soul, and it rises to the cognitive level of the mind. Deep inside, we know intuitively that all wisdom, knowledge, and truth are within us; right at our fingertips, we have access to the cosmic encyclopedia of life. The journey we embark on now will allow us to activate these seeds. Known as the Jesus seeds, the awakening of this wisdom within us is through the touch or vibration of divine grace.

Allowing ourselves to be open to divine grace and consciously committing to our evolution prepare us to be awash in divine wisdom. This insight allows us to understand that evolution is a two-way street: it is the willingness and eagerness of the soul to touch the Divine, and the ever-mysterious grace of the Divine reaching to reignite the soul. Sloughing off the blanket of amnesia, the soul receives the divine frequency or vibration and drinks like a man lost in the desert and dying from thirst. The engorgement of the soul with the divine vibration accelerates our evolution.

The soul pushes to the forefront of the personality and takes the lead on the journey to evolve. When we are open to learning, new ideas and experiences are like rocket fuel to the soul. This divine push, or jump-start, propels us to move further into previously unknown states of awareness. The jump—or sometimes leap—into new levels of consciousness opens us to the miracles of the ages. When the miracles begin, the evolutionary journey becomes a self-fulfilling prophecy. The previously unbelievable becomes not only believable, but it is also our new reality.

As we build this new worldview, we will find that the process may not be linear. We are conditioned to believe that construction requires a brick-by-brick building of reality—but what if we do not need to labor with the bricks? What if we can imagine and then manifest? What if we can imagine what is needed and then *effortlessly* manifest with God's grace? This may seem impossible, because we are used to toiling and expending large amounts of energy to create. What if we shift this thinking to a new level of awareness? What would life be like if we could engage in manifesting our world in an instant rather than struggling with the bricks? Let's see what this life could be and what we need to embrace to achieve this new worldview.

The Creation

All of creation begins with the breath. Inspiration is the movement of the God-force into your body. When you feel the rush of the molecules into the lungs, the energy dissipates throughout the cells into the molecular building blocks of our existence. Exhalation brings the spirit of creation from within us out to the universe around us.

This ever-present cycle of receiving and giving of the life force illustrates our perpetual links to the Divine. *Ruach*, a Hebrew word meaning "divine spirit," infiltrates our bodies and minds to the subtlest levels of the microcosm. Awareness of the breath and her permeation of our being brings our attention to the present moment.

Present moment awareness is the pinnacle of God's presence. When we afford ourselves the luxury of single-minded presence, we can open to the vast glory of Christ consciousness. Many meditations of Eastern origin focus our awareness on the breath. Using this technique, we can focus

11

our attention on this moment, the present moment. The present moment does not contain the past or the future; it only captures the eternal present moment, the precise portal into multiple dimensions. Going deeper into the present moment allows us to delve deeper into Christ consciousness. This divine level of awareness is ever-present—we simply have to become aware of its presence.

Jesus said, "The Kingdom is within you and it is outside of you."[1] He was speaking of the ever-present Christ consciousness. Abiding in Christ consciousness is being in the kingdom of heaven. Heaven is not some faraway place one can only travel to after death. Heaven exists here—today. Heaven is the eternal immersion of the soul in the frequency of Christ consciousness.

The soul vibrates inherently at the level of Christ consciousness. When born into the physical density of a human body, she forgets her natural state of existence; she sees the three-dimensional view of our earth and believes this is her only reality. The soul understands where she is but has a deeper longing for a connection that seems lost. She will spend her lifetime seeking this last piece of herself, knowing all along that there is more, that more is possible.

The connection to kingdom consciousness is what the soul is longing for, what she seeks and knows at her core is possible. Trying to communicate the deep longing of this essential need in words is difficult. Language can be a barrier to fully expressing our needs and experiences. Let's call this deep-seated longing for immersion in kingdom consciousness our birthright.

---

[1] Davies, *The Gospel of Thomas*, p. 5.

Our birth into a physical body places us in a density paradigm of a lower frequency than before our birth. The soul vibrates at a much higher frequency before she arrives in the physical body. It is the lowering of the soul's frequency from kingdom consciousness pre-birth to earthly consciousness post-birth that gives rise to this longing for kingdom consciousness, the frequency of home.

Understanding that kingdom consciousness, or Christ consciousness, is our birthright may seem appalling to some members of society. However, our souls know at their deepest level that this is our truth, our home, and our birthright. Known by many names, including Krishna consciousness and Buddha nature, this level of consciousness or frequency resonates within every soul. The secret is to let this frequency radiate out from us to all of those around us. This is the primary tenant of our birthright. Let the frequency of your soul radiate throughout the world.

Let's think about this for a minute. Each person is born with the birthright to vibrate at the frequency of Christ consciousness. At this level of vibration, the soul dances in Christ consciousness, radiating like the sun in all directions. This level of consciousness emits love, health, abundance, prosperity, joy, and peace to all it touches. If this level of consciousness is our birthright, why are we all not currently vibrating at this level? Why are we not dancing in kingdom consciousness? Why are we not insisting that this right, given to us at birth, be *activated?*

There are many levels to unravel to reach the answers to these questions. The simplest answer is that we have forgotten our brilliance and our birthright. Before we are born, the angels tell us that we will discover a great secret when we are born, but that we will not remember it right away. The angels lightly touch our faces between the nose and chin, leaving us with a small cradle beneath our noses. This cradle reminds us that the secret will be found right under our noses when we wake up. Ironic as this paradox is, when we once again realize that we always had and always will have the ability to vibrate at the Christ consciousness frequency, we will laugh at the fact that we actually forgot this secret.

What does it take to reclaim our birthright? What can we do to reignite Christ consciousness in our lives? How do we jump-start the remembrance of this vibration and create heaven on earth? The first step involves recognition.

Recognizing the Divine Within

With every breath we take, the soul begs us to remember our divinity. The Holy Spirit, inhaled as an elixir of potential, washes through us and beckons the flame of remembrance to ignite. However, our day-to-day existence counters this potential and sweeps it away as we focus on worldly goods and desires. We are continually drowned in external stimuli, moving our awareness in a multitude of directions. In addition, our minds generally look to the past or plan a future—anywhere but the present moment.

The leap from everyday awareness to kingdom consciousness takes place in the blink of an eye. As Jesus described, a fish swimming in water is not aware of the water. Likewise, we are surrounded by Christ consciousness and are not even aware of it. Thus, the recognition takes place in the blink of an eye, because it is always there. Christ consciousness is. Kingdom consciousness is. It is already within you and around you; you just have to recognize, or re-cognize, its existence. To understand it requires knowledge of it and the experience of it. How do we find kingdom consciousness?

Knowledge of Christ consciousness is easy to obtain. Thousands of books have been written, extolling the virtues and characteristics of Christ consciousness. Love, peace, prosperity, joy, abundance, and vitality are just some of the facets this level of awareness manifests. Saints and sages provide wisdom-filled quotes in an effort to convey the experience of Christ consciousness. However, we know that words limit the expression of our experiences. To distill an extraordinary experience into a word made up of consonants and vowels constricts the expansiveness and depth of an experience. The true experience of Christ consciousness is in our bodies.

Sri Aurobindo spoke of the divinization of the human being. The ability of the human body to be the conduit of energy between the earth and the heavens affords us the opportunity to experience Christ consciousness. The vibration of Christ consciousness is higher than our everyday level of vibration; it is the density and lower vibration of the body that deceives the soul into believing that she needs to vibrate at this lower level of existence. The soul longs for a higher vibration and always seeks this avenue of expansion. When given an opportunity to experience this higher frequency, the soul gushes with remembrance of what is possible, and the quest for a higher level of vibration is initiated.

Like the knights of King Arthur's Round Table, the soul pledges to seek and find reconnection with Christ consciousness. This sacred quest envelops the soul as she strives to become fully emerged in the vibration of kingdom consciousness. The secret has been revealed. Christ consciousness is our true nature;

it is the soul's responsibility to awaken this potential in the body. This awakening is what Sri Ramakrishna refers to when he says once you are awakened, you will search for the Divine like a man whose hair is on fire seeks a pond. The urgency of this desire to reunite with Christ consciousness swells into an overabundance of lust to taste this level of vibration again. And so, the quest begins.

The Quest

In King Arthur's court, the knights of the Round Table were tasked with finding the Holy Grail. Each knight took an oath and pledged to dedicate his life to seeking the Holy Grail, and once found, to serve the purpose found in the Holy Grail. There were two questions the knights would ask the Holy Grail when it was found. First, whom does the Grail serve? Second, what is the meaning of life? It is these answers that would guide the knights for the rest of their days.

Similarly, when the soul is awakened, she knows the quest has begun. Her longing cannot be diminished by earthly treasures, but rather it demands the heavenly wisdom of her potential. In seeking, she finds the Holy Grail and can ask her questions to support her quest.

Whom does the Grail serve? *The light of God, the highest vibration.*

What is the meaning of life? *To serve the light.*

With these answers, the soul knows she seeks the highest vibration of kingdom consciousness as her quest. Like a fish swimming in water, she must bring conscious awareness of the vibration of Christ consciousness to the body for recognition.

Bringing the Vibration Home

By looking at the human body as a microcosm of the universal macrocosm, we find the evolutionary steps required to move beyond our current form in the secret of vibration. On the earth plane of existence, the density keeps us in a holding pattern. We continually circle the activities of our day in the same level of awareness. Our quest, if we choose to accept it, is to move to successively higher levels of awareness. Think of it like Jacob's ladder. In his dream, Jacob saw a ladder going from earth to the heavens. On the ladder, he saw angels climbing up to heaven. Like the angels, we can climb each rung of the ladder and, with each step, raise our level of vibration.

Raising our level of vibration allows us to simultaneously access higher dimensional reality. There are untold levels of awareness and corresponding levels of vibrational frequency. Every soul has its own path to kingdom consciousness. It is said there are as many paths to God as there are grains of sand on all the beaches in the world; with this as our compass, every soul's guide map is different. However, there will be a commonality to some experiences, and thus we will chart a new language to navigate our individual paths to Christ consciousness.

To think about different levels of consciousness and our experience in each level, let's compare three levels of consciousness we are all familiar with—deep sleep, dreaming, and the awake state. In deep sleep, our consciousness appears to be dulled, and little remembrance of this experience rises to the level of our awareness. In the dream state, our consciousness is more aware as we participate in dreams. We may or may not be aware of our dreams when we wake up, but sometimes we can remember the stories of our subconscious. In the awake state, we are fully aware of our surroundings, remember some of our dreams, and usually have no recollection of the deep sleep state. Each of the three levels of awareness is essential for our health. However, the experience of each level is very different.

Let's take this a step further. We have all had experiences of different levels of awareness. When we discuss how we felt in each level or state of awareness, our stories will have common threads but will also be vastly different in viewpoint, explanations, and individual experience. If we take this same paradigm and apply it to the untold number of states of awareness available for us to explore, we can see how it would be helpful to build a vocabulary around our experiences so that we can share our quest for the higher vibration of Christ consciousness with others.

Raising our vibration literally means just that: raising the vibration of every part of our existence, raising the vibration of each cell in our bodies, raising the vibration of every thought in our minds, and raising the vibration of the environment around us. These different areas of our life are not separate but are rather intricately interwoven. As such, a change in one aspect of our existence will impact all areas of our lives. As we begin to chart our paths to higher realms of awareness, it is essential that we keep the interconnected nature of existence as a primary tenant of our evolution. As my body changes, my thoughts change; as my thoughts change, my environment changes. As all of these change, my level of vibration changes.

In deep sleep, dreaming, and awake states of awareness, we do not find ourselves in one level of consciousness at all times. We move between these states of awareness. I wake up in the morning and spend my day in the awake state. In the evening, I transition to the dream state and then move into deep sleep states throughout the night. This cycle of awareness is a continuous shifting of our consciousness and level of vibration.

As we begin to consciously experience higher levels of vibration, our experiences will change. The characteristics of each level of vibration are different and thus our experiences are different. This is the excitement in the quest. Like Christopher Columbus exploring new worlds, we will explore new vibratory worlds. In each new world, our experiences will be different. Naturally, we may feel fear in opening ourselves to the unknown. The unknown is only the unknown until we experience it and expand our worldview to include it. Then the unknown, or the miraculous, becomes part of our everyday reality.

This is the quest that we begin together. In this journey, we will develop a new language to capture our experiences so we can contextualize them into our daily conversations. Imagine

The Vibratory Scale

When we think about the vibratory scale, we can liken it to a musical scale. Each note on the scale has a specific frequency that makes a certain sound. Individually, the notes stand as frequencies that, when combined, create music. The frequency of the notes can be felt in our bodies, our minds perceive the sound, and the environment resonates with the frequency of the vibration. Similarly, our experience of various levels of vibration also has multiple parts. As we experience higher levels of vibration, our bodies will feel the effect, the perception of our minds will change, and the environment around us will shift as the frequency increases.

It is this triumvirate of experience that we will chart on this course. "What am I feeling in my body? What am I perceiving with my mind? What changes are occurring in my environment?" Not to be too scientific about our explorations, but an observational methodology will assist us in both navigating new worlds and developing the language so we can talk to others as we communally move through a shift to higher levels of vibration.

The book *A Course of Miracles* begins with the following assertion: "There is no order of difficulty in miracles."[1] A miracle is an ordinary experience; we simply perceive what we call a miracle to be a rare and exceptional occurrence. What if we raised our awareness and vibration to a level where a miracle was an everyday occurrence? Jesus said, "When you say, Move mountain!, it will move."[2] How is this possible? This would be a miracle. If we are in a state of Christ consciousness, this would not be a miracle but rather a fact. My verbal commands create a vibrational code that, in a higher state of awareness, manifests as requested.

Allow yourself to take in this concept for a moment and ponder the consequences. In Genesis, we are given the proverbial words of creation. "In the beginning, the Lord God said, *Let there be light*, and there was light."[3] The vibration of the spoken word is the creationary impulse in this dimension. The vibration gives form to mass, which manifests as density. With this formula, we can create our reality through the spoken word.

In Dr. Masaru Emoto's work with water crystals, we can see the brilliance of kind words, prayers, and uplifting music as they form exquisite water crystals captured in time. It is the fundamental vibration that serves as the energetic building

---

[1] *A Course in Miracles* (New York, Penguin Books, 1975), p. 3.

[2] Davies, *The Gospel of Thomas*, p. 129.

[3] Gen. 1:3. (AV)

blocks for the crystals. The molecules form to intricately align with the vibration of the energetic impulse. The manifestation of invisible impulses into crystal creations illustrates a concrete example of how words, music, and prayer create structure in our environment.

In our next stage of evolution, we must become acutely aware of the power of our words and use them to create an uplifted society rather than to destroy. We must not only step into our power but also accept the responsibility we inherit as our divine birthright. Looking at this responsibility, we now face the truth of our creative ownership for the reality known as kingdom consciousness.

A New Reality

To step into the realm of Christ consciousness, we need to suspend judgment of what is possible, because limited perceptions constrict our expansion into a new existence. Cognitively we are raised within a paradigm of what is physically possible and what is not possible; given these parameters, we live our lives within the walls of lack and limitation. Shifting to a multidimensional view of reality will involve breaking down the walls of our current worldview and stepping through to a new potential.

The major paradigm shifts in the history of humanity have been hard won. When Columbus proved the world was not flat, seafaring exploration expanded. When the Wright brothers proved winged flight was possible, aviation changed our world. When electron microscopes proved that atoms were not the smallest particles of matter and that electrons, protons and neutrons existed, our world changed.

We find ourselves at a critical point in history where physicists have shown that multiple dimensions exist. Doesn't the next logical step then beg us to explore these dimensions? We exist today in a three-dimensional worldview. What if we elevate our worldview to contain a fifth-dimensional view? What if we expand our awareness to live in a *multidimensional universe?* What new course of action would be possible? How would our lives change? Let's explore what this new awareness can bring to our evolutionary potential and how Christ consciousness will seem more attainable.

Seeing the World through God's Eyes

Omnipotent. Omniscient. What do these words have in common? *Omni,* or *one,* is the answer: one view of creation as it is unfolding. In the eternal present moment, there is one view of all existence. This is why God is called omniscient. Seeing reality from a multidimensional view allows all things to be seen simultaneously. This multifaceted, multilayered view affords the individual soul the ability to see God's grace in all of existence. The soul as your light, your beacon of God's greatness, looks out of your eyes and sees a three-dimensional world. This worldview is constrained by what the mind believes to be true and then sculpts its reality. However, the soul, being multidimensional in nature, can see more than the mind can perceive. It is at this point where we can purposefully take steps to expand our minds to allow the soul to cognize multidimensional reality through our eyes.

Here is an example. It has been reported that when the Spanish conquistadors arrived in Central America, the indigenous people could not perceive the ships in the Spanish fleet; the concept of a floating vessel as large as a ship had not been physically seen before by the native people. However, as the experience of the large ships unfolded, the worldview shifted, allowing a new experience to be understood and perceived by the indigenous population. This shift in cognition allowed an expanded worldview. From that point forward, the Central American native people lived in a world where Spanish ships existed. Although this is one small example of the possible shift in human cognition, it can be used to illustrate how kingdom consciousness exists. It exists within and around us at all time—we simply have to expand our awareness to be able to perceive it.

As we collectively take our next step in human evolution, seeing the world from a multidimensional viewpoint will be commonplace. Being able to see the world through God's eyes is a gift that God gives to each of us as we take our first breath at birth. God-sight is our birthright. It is our divinity birthed in a human body. God-sight is our natural state of consciousness in his kingdom. However, as we grow up in a world that conforms to three-dimensional rules and precepts, we lose our God-sight and fall into complacency because we do not know any better. We believe we are living life to the fullest, but we have long forgotten our God-sight potential.

As we evolve from three-dimensional to multidimensional sight, we only need to remember that God-sight is our birthright. We were born with this native ability, and so we can remember this capability exists and resurrect it. The soul knows we have this ability. She is here to guide you along the path of remembering.

She uses a tool called intuition to navigate the evolutionary pathway to remembrance of your magnificence. One step on this re-connective path is the acceptance of your God-sight. Let the unfurling of your greatness begin.

The Greater Now

In our perception, it appears that we have a collection of experiences that comprise our past and the unformed dreams of the future. We compartmentalize our experiences and segregate them into discrete packets of time. When looking at this through God's eyes, the discretionary packets dissolve because all events occur simultaneously, without the constraint of space and time.

When we move to higher dimensional consciousness, the frequencies allow us to peer beyond third-dimensional constraints of space and time. The space-time continuum fades, and all is occurring simultaneously in one orchestrated moment. This is the Greater Now. When we say that God is omniscient, we are saying that the ability to see all exists at a divine level of consciousness. Think about this word. Omniscient: one view of all there is. This is the Greater Now.

When released from the constraints of third-dimensional reality, we step into the light of kingdom consciousness. In greater expanses of light, we can see more and cognize more than we thought possible. It is like shining a flashlight across a room. In a dark room, we would only see a small path of light cutting through the darkness. However, if we turn on the overhead light in a room, we can see everything in the room, even to the farthest corners. Using this same concept, let's think about shining divine light on our worldview. What if we could illuminate our lives so that we could see to the ends of the universe and beyond? What if we could infuse our lives with so much divine light that we began to see our past, present, and future as one? What if we could step into the Greater Now, the kingdom consciousness that is our birthright?

Many philosophers and spiritual teachers speak of the Greater Now, the present moment of experience. The present moment is when your inhalation brings your focus to your breath. The present moment is when your exhalation firmly anchors you in this moment of existence. This is the gateway to kingdom consciousness. This is the portal we walk through to claim our birthright. This is the doorway we have been searching for. Let's step through the doorway and explore what is waiting for us; let us explore what is calling us to become our higher selves.

The Calling

I t is said that every soul is called by God. Every human being has and will have again the experience of being called. It is that unmistakable moment when we understand there is more to this earthly reality than we can see. It is a deep longing to reconnect with our homeland, to go back to where we came from, to feel the sacred touch of God. This calling urges us to take a step off our current paths and march boldly on a new course. It feels right. It feels enriching. It feels scary.

The fear arises as a rebuttal to the overwhelming love that we know is possible. In this third-dimensional existence, we live in a constant state of dualistic experiences: love and fear, good and bad, right and wrong. This dualistic expressionism allows our minds to categorize our reality so that choices can be made. This consciousness of duality is the lowest working expression of our abilities as human beings. To unlock our potential, we must move beyond duality to a higher level of awareness where singularity exists. The splitting of consciousness into duality limits our ability to interpret reality as a unified expression of existence.

Reflected by the two hemispheres of the brain, our dual nature propagates a limited worldview. The corpus callosum, which connects the two sides of our brains, is the conjunctive pathway to unity consciousness. Our ability to move from dual hemispheres to a unified mind meld of one view of reality provides us with the God-view of experience. Omniscience is one unified understanding of reality, one cosmic glimpse of existence.

To move beyond duality, we must shift our conceptual analysis of the world from "either/or" to "both/and" perception. The either/or comprehension is inherently limiting and perpetuates the constraints of our reality. The both/and expanded understanding opens us to walk a larger path. We step off the current path onto an unlimited path to follow the calling of our God-nature—to walk boldly where no man has walked before, as our Star Trek brethren would say: to explore unknown universes beyond our galaxy and to be the galactic explorer speeding to meet his maker in higher dimensional awareness, to step into kingdom consciousness and reunite with our fullest truth and potential. Here is where our journeys begin.

PART II

—◦◦◦—

Recognize what is right in front
of you, and that which is hidden
from you will be revealed. Nothing
hidden will fail to be displayed.

—Jesus Christ

The Next Chapter

As we look to the future, we know it is time to turn the page and begin the next chapter of our existence. We look around and see the beauty of potential and the madness of reality. Knowing we can be more, our souls are screaming to get our attention through the dense fog of electronic bombardment. Our lives are filled from morning to night with noise: television, the Internet, conversation, congested traffic. Where is our moment of silence? When do we give ourselves the opportunity to connect with and listen to our souls?

Our souls communicate with us through subtle vibrations. This energetic transmission manifests as intuition, thoughts, feelings, visions, and a deep sense of knowing. How can the soul compete with the external noise when her message is shared internally in quiet grace and ease? We need to shift our behaviors to allow time for our *soul connection*, a daily chance for her wisdom to infiltrate our lives. A few minutes of silence each day to allow her message to reach our conscious awareness and guide our evolution. The key to conscious evolution is to surrender to her ultimate wisdom. As a spark of the Godhead, our souls have the infinite playbook for our existence. She has the plays that will expand our knowingness, enhance our vitality, and leverage our God-given gifts to blossom into their full potential.

Each person on earth has God-given gifts that are destined to be birthed during our lifetimes. These inherent gifts glimmer under the surface of our awareness. It is our responsibility to ensure the brilliance breaks through the surface of awareness so that the gifts are released into the world. The conscious manifestation of our gifts allows our contributions to escalate the birth of the kingdom of heaven on earth. The emergence and anchoring of Christ consciousness requires active and conscious participation to make this a permanent shift.

Examples of human beings living in kingdom consciousness abound throughout the ages. Jesus, Buddha, and Krishna lived in Christ consciousness, Buddha consciousness, and Krishna consciousness while on earth. Their lives are examples of what is possible if we allow ourselves to step forward into our truest form of existence. We may need to collectively give ourselves permission to step into this new consciousness. We may need to hold hands with others as we face the fear of the unknown. We may need support to step into a world that is beyond imagining: grace-filled, abundant, vital, loving, and peaceful.

Whatever it takes, we need to do it. Holding hands, jumping, crawling, crying, kicking, screaming—no matter what, we need to move forward. This collective step forward is right there for us. We simply need to lift our feet and then plant them firmly in our destiny. Would it help to ease the fear if we could understand-what waits for us on the other side? The ability to understand the potential that awaits may be difficult to comprehend because words are so limited in their ability to convey an experience. Be that as it may, let's try to articulate the experience by building a new language that we can use to interpret our experiences as well as share them with others. Every year *Webster's Dictionary* adds new words to the English language. These words emerge from society as new technologies, fashions, and trends are introduced. Similarly, let's work together to identify a new language to communicate our collective experiences as we begin the next chapter together.

Hieroglyphics

When wandering the massive remnants of the Egyptian empire, you are bombarded with a pictographic representation of sacred symbols, each expressing a deeply evolved communicative story of an experience. To the inexperienced eye, the hieroglyphs seem like cryptic symbols whose secrets cannot be unlocked. We need a key to unlock the meaning of the symbols. The Rosetta stone is the key to translating and aligning language so a common conversation can be initiated. We need to develop a similar *Rosetta stone of consciousness* that will allow us to speak of our experiences in kingdom consciousness and anchor this level of consciousness in our daily lives.

The impulses we receive from our souls are known as soul codes. Deep within the soul are individual codes that blossom to propel us into our greatness. The process to vibrationally unwrap the gift of our soul codes is the simple act of silence. Our souls communicate through subtle vibration; her energetic impulses can be received and comprehended through our nervous system. The energetic impulses arise in our conscious awareness as the transmissions pulsate through our beings. The impulses are then translated into feelings, intuition, visions, and messages that generate understanding through our minds and senses. When the soul impulses are received and translated, the communication is then cognized in the mind, and the movement of messages from the soul to the mind is complete. Once the message is received, we are then responsible for acting on it. Through this process of soul communication, her directions can be implemented in this third-dimensional reality.

Think about this: a higher dimensional communication from our souls is transmitted to our third-dimensional consciousness, and then we have a choice to act on this personalized guidance. What could be simpler? We are given clear, personalized guidance from our souls to illicit actions that will unleash our greatest potential. We are receiving impulses of genius that stimulate the giving of our God-given gifts to the world. We are being offered a clear road map to greatness, which we only need to follow as we re-cognize our higher selves. This, my friends, is how we anchor kingdom consciousness on earth.

If every soul on earth would open to their inherent magnificence and step into kingdom consciousness, we would all benefit from a collective shift that is unprecedented in human history. How do we work together to make this happen? One soul at a time. We each take personal responsibility to consciously connect with our souls and fully engage in the roadmap to our divine destiny. This grace-filled surrender to our divine plan will allow us to achieve our potential to live in heaven on earth. The divine orchestration of soul road maps to culminate in a shift to higher consciousness for all mankind is beyond brilliant—it is omniscient.

Connecting with the Soul

At the onset of the soul opening, the mind questions the shift in the psyche. The ego, having led the charge for the first part of a person's life, questions the presence of a higher authority. This soul essence flows through the mind and body, permeating every cell. As the mind and body awaken to the soul's energy, the feelings are abundantly clear that the person has found her way home. The ambience inculcates the person with such a deep knowingness that its right-ness cannot be denied. However, the ego does not see it that way.

The transition from ego-based living to soul-guided existence is perfected through a series of cognitive shifts. At first the ego will refuse to take a back seat to the soul. Having always been in charge, the soul has operated behind a veil, allowing the ego to believe that it has been the commander from day one. When the time comes for the soul to lift the veil and step in as the cosmic commander, the ego typically does not take this shift in power very well.

The ego questions the emergence of the new energy and, feeling unsettled, rebels against this force. The mind spins in disbelief, questioning the validity of what is happening. The ego fights to keep what is his or hers, drawing a line in the sand and refusing to shift or release its perceived authority. Unfortunately for the ego, the soul knows how to move the sands of time and will continue to gently brush aside the arguments of the mind. Ultimately, the ego will move to the background, and the soul takes the reins as the new leader. The ego will not willingly take a back seat, but when the soul surges to the front of our awareness, the ego understands that an understudy role is better than no role at all.

When the soul moves to the forefront of our conscious awareness and the ego takes a secondary seat, the mind can feel as if it has been possessed by a foreign entity. The shift in energy and vibration that the soul brings to the surface feels completely right, yet completely strange. Words of truth and compassion emerge in a finite clarity, giving pause to the mind as it integrates the new perspective. Like a child learning to walk, the mind learns to articulate the messages from the soul. Although what emerges from the soul in both thought and speech may be surprising at first, with more time and practice, the transition is completed with grace and ease.

Meanwhile, the ego, having taken a back seat to the soul, continues to exist but finds its influence greatly diminished. Not one to give up easily, the ego will try to climb into the front seat from time to time. When it does, the soul will observe this movement and escort the ego back to a secondary role. Over time, we can actually feel this interplay between the soul force and the ego. As we begin to cognize the subtle differences between soul speak and ego demands, we will recognize how we are responding in our daily interactions. The ability to observe this difference in our thoughts, feelings, words, and deeds gives us a profound opportunity to not only embrace the change occurring within us, but to also see how this change impacts the world around us.

As Mahatma Gandhi said, "We must be the change we wish to see in the world." The change from an ego-driven to soul-guided life is a cornerstone to walking forth into the beingness of Christ consciousness. Once we are anchored in the choice to accept the soul as our internal commander, then we can move forward into raising the vibration of our existence.

Vibrational Density

As we prepare our bodies to be the receptacle for Christ consciousness, we need to understand the precise requirements for our evolution. Christ revealed that the kingdom of God is within you. He is telling us that we are the keepers of kingdom consciousness, the temple that holds the vibration of Christ consciousness.

To unveil this vibration in our bodies, we must prepare ourselves to be able to hold this level of consciousness. In a vibratory multidimensional universe, it is the rate or frequency of vibration that differentiates our ability to experience various dimensions. As we explored previously, every level of frequency opens us to different fields of experience. The consciousness we experience in deep sleep is different from the dream state, which differs significantly from our everyday awake state. Let's take this analogy one step further. The everyday awake state will have different properties and experiences than a higher vibratory dimension of Christ consciousness. The rules of what can and cannot be in the ordinary, everyday awake state are shattered when we enter the higher dimensional state of Christ consciousness. Jesus taught that we will be able to do what he did, and even more. He knew the potential that resides inside of us to experience and live in Christ consciousness, to do more than even he himself could do. With the gauntlet being thrown down, as knights of kingdom consciousness, we must continue on the quest to raise our vibratory existence. Let's explore what this journey will entail and continue to move forward.

In our bodies, we store energy at different levels of vibrational density. Throughout our lives, each emotional experience contains a certain vibratory signature. Depending on the density of the vibrational signature and our emotional processing of the event, some emotional experiences move through our energy fields while others are trapped. It is the denser vibrational emotional blocks that we need to release from our energy fields. These denser vibrations impede our evolutionary progress in raising our overall vibration to the level of Christ consciousness.

Body-quakes are body-shaking movements that release dense vibrational energies. When the density is stuck in our energy channels, it is the body movement that facilitates the release of the blockage. However, this release is not as easy as just shaking our bodies; it also involves the intentional emotional release of the blockage as well as the movement of the breath to shift the vibrational density out of our energy fields.

If we think of each of the emotional density blockages as a road block to allowing a higher level of vibrational energy to move through us, it makes sense that we need to remove any impediment required to allow the energy of Christ consciousness to easily flow through us. Think of it as a giant, energetic Roto-Rooter used to cleanse the energy field of all emotional debris clogging our energy pathways. When all the debris is cleared away, the energy can flow freely and uninterrupted. This is when the energy of kingdom consciousness can reside in our temples of physical form.

The Continuum of Change

I n every evolutionary pattern, there is a point in time when a giant leap occurs. Evolution is not linear but rather accelerates through the benefit of quantum leaps. Look at the change in computers over the past decade: leaps not even imaginable ten years ago are overshadowed by significant developments each year.

We are engaged in a quantum leap to the next level of our potentiality. With unlimited boundaries, we are now being asked to take a step forward that will change everything we know; it is the proverbial game changer, a change so massive yet so realistic that to struggle against it seems like a cosmic joke.

We believe that we have it all figured out. We know the truth, we know our world, and we know our capacity. Science establishes the boundaries of reality as our Darwinian indoctrination limits what is possible. Now we are being asked to take a quantum leap that may not be explained by scientific precepts of what is real and what is fantasy. We are going to join hands and carry ourselves, our families, and our friends over a threshold of change so quickly mastered that once we are on the other side, we will look back and laugh at why we made such a fuss at taking our first steps.

All monumental change is at first met with resistance. Why? It is because change means moving into a space of uncertainty, a place of unknowing, a time where boundaries melt, allowing for new boundaries to be erected. The resistance at first will be strong, driven by fear. Over time, the power of God's grace will ease each soul into the space of kingdom consciousness with such love that the receptivity will overwhelm any resistance. God's love permeates the soul and radiates through the body and mind, triggering the remembrance of what is possible. The remembrance of what is possible shatters the fear, doubt, and resistance to change.

As we make this quantum leap together, remember to embrace God's grace; allow it to permeate every cell in your body and every atom in your mind. The expansion of this energy has been predicted by the sages for centuries. We are the chosen ones who are being given the chance to lead this shift in human consciousness that will fuel the quantum leap in our evolution. How can we say no to the greatest gift ever afforded to mankind? Saying no is simply not an option—not to a wayfaring species driven by courage, propelled by love, and guided by the hand of grace. Our destiny awaits.

Seeing a New Future

S ages of old and new alike have prognosticated on what the future may be, on what our collective destiny will be. Given the new paradigm, however, there is no future to predict, only a present moment to explore. The symmetry of the present moment and the impact of this concept on our evolution cannot be overstated. In fact, let's delve into it further to defy what our logical minds tell us is so. Let's push ourselves to a new level of thinking, in order to explore and experience at the same time.

Give yourself a moment to take a really deep breath that makes your stomach puff out and stretches your ribs. Now, let this deep breath leave your body, allowing your lungs to relax at their own pace. Engage in this relaxed breathing for several minutes, allowing your body to relax and your breath to flow. As you engage in this deep breathing, very gently focus your mind on the breath. This is a simple exercise. Breathe in and focus on your breath; breathe out and focus on the air leaving your body. Continue in this state until you can feel your muscles relaxing and your mind focused on the breath.

Once you are in breath awareness mode, ask yourself this question: "Is there a future?" Sit with this question in silence for a moment as you continue to focus on your breath.

Now ask yourself, "Is there a past?" Continue to breathe. Listen to the stillness of your heart. As you continue to focus on your breath, you will come to realize that this breath is all there is. This breath connects us to the present moment, the only moment that exists.

The past is filled with thoughts, actions, and deeds that no longer exist. The future is a fantasy-filled illusion of what may manifest. In all truth, the only moment that truly exists is the present moment. It is through the breath that we connect with the present moment—and in the present moment, we connect with Christ consciousness.

This gateway or portal to Christ consciousness has always existed; we are simply distracted by thoughts or judgments about the past and a preconceived notion of what the future holds. The truest expression of our oneness with Christ consciousness occurs when we connect with the breath and allow the essence of pure spirit to vibrate within us. This vibration that connects with and permeates each cell in our bodies is our natural state of being. In this vibration, we feel happy, healthy, and whole. This primal resonance touches the deepest core of our existence and awakens the remembrance of our wholeness. It reminds us of what it feels like to be home in kingdom consciousness.

Our Home, Our Kingdom

I n the quest for the Holy Grail, the knights of the Round
Table took an oath to persevere in their quest until they
found the Grail or died during the journey to which they
were bound. The irony is that no amount of seeking or searching
will lead us to the Holy Grail, because the treasure is not outside
of us. The treasure is inside of us.

The five physical senses interpret external stimuli that
convince us from an early age that all treasure is outside
of us. The sights, sounds, tastes, touches, and smells of the
external world captivate our awareness and draw our attention
outside of us. This cognitive dissonance propels us down an
external path of seeking, rather than the internal world of Christ
consciousness.

The outer world continually stimulates our senses to reinforce
the external search. When we shift to consciously look inside,
at first we find the noise of thoughts and the energetics of
emotions. This constant swirl makes it appear that our internal

dialogue is as rampant as the external stimuli we encounter every day. But here is the secret: if we can focus on the breath and allow the thoughts and emotions to fade away, we can use the gateway of the breath to access kingdom consciousness. In the gospel of Thomas, Jesus said, "The seeker should not stop until he finds. When he does find, he will be disturbed. After having been disturbed, he will be astonished. Then he will reign over everything."[1]

In this gospel, Jesus highlights the stages of the seeker's quest. He encourages us to seek and warns that we will be disturbed by what we find. Once we integrate the disturbance, we will be in awe. When we focus on the breath, we see very intimately the thoughts that race through the mind. We begin to realize the repetitive and redundant stream of thoughts that capture our awareness and hold it hostage in either a past that no longer exists or a future that has not been created. The energy that it takes to maintain the stories of our past and the preconceived nature of our future traps us in a repetitive cycle of limited growth. The same stories play over and over again, telling us who we are and limiting our potential for new growth. When we focus on the breath, these thoughts rise to the level of our conscious awareness, and the reaction can be disturbing. "Is this what I am thinking about all day long? Am I really thinking about that over and over again? Can I actually be spending most of my waking hours obsessing over this?"

Once we become aware of our thoughts, we do become disturbed. This is nothing compared to how disturbed we will be when the emotions begin to arise. As we continue to focus

---

[1] Davies, *The Gospel of Thomas*, p. 3.

on the breath, we see the thoughts that fill our minds both day and night. This non-stop river of thoughts continues to flow, relentless in motion and disturbing in content. If we continue to focus on the breath and allow the thoughts to flow without attachment and judgment, we will find that our emotional stories begin to rise into our conscious awareness.

The body continues to relax as we breathe. With each breath, we allow the frenetic activity of the mind to relinquish its grip on our conscious awareness. If we continue this practice, we find that emotions begin to arise from our bodies, from deep within our cellular memory. It is these emotional memories that cause an even greater disturbance in our reality.

In the midst of focusing on the breath, emotional memories from childhood through our adult years arise. We feel the energy of pain, abandonment, unworthiness, fear, anger, and rage emanate from deep within us. As these emotional stories arise, we glimpse in them the most intimate places in our history, and we are disturbed.

If we continue to focus on the breath as these emotions arise, we will be disturbed as the feelings move through our bodies. However, once the emotion has moved through the body, and we consciously witness the experience, the energy associated with the emotion dissipates. The energy is released, which allows us to be amazed at the clearing we feel inside.

This is the simple process that Jesus so eloquently describes in the gospel of Thomas. We seek outside of ourselves until we realize that the breath is our connection to Christ consciousness. Once we focus our awareness on the breath, we become fully aware of the thoughts that occupy our minds. When we release attachment to and judgment of these thoughts, we open ourselves to allow our emotional stories to arise. In allowing emotions to arise, the energy trapped by the emotions in our bodies is released. This allows for an opening, a spaciousness within us. It is this opening that allows the energy of Christ consciousness to fill us full to the brim.

When we are filled with Christ consciousness, we find ourselves at the end of our seeking. We find ourselves in the realm of kingdom consciousness. It is then that we know we are home. Once we are home in the kingdom, we shall reign with divine grace, relax into Christ's love, and breathe evermore in alignment with our authentic nature. Now we can relax before we take the next step into what is possible when we exist in kingdom consciousness.

Living in the Kingdom

Jesus was very explicit when he spoke of our potential in the kingdom. In kingdom consciousness, our abilities expand far beyond what we know or understand as possible today. When Jesus walked the earth, his ability to heal the sick and perform miracles astounded his followers and non-followers alike. In healing the sick, he restored the natural balance of their bodies. In walking on water, he proved that the perceived laws of nature could be broken. In raising the dead, he proved the eternal existence of the soul and the activation of the Holy Spirit within the body. In each miracle, Jesus taught us a lesson: the basis of our core beliefs is incorrect. There is more potential within and around us than we understand.

He tells us that we can do what he can do, and more. What will it take for us to believe this statement? We have to suspend our beliefs, open our hearts, and be willing to step out of our comfort zone to walk a new path. The path to kingdom consciousness brings with it the keys to our Christed potential.

The indoctrination of our youth must be shattered so that we can take the quantum leap to this new level of reality, where miracles are commonplace and love drives our actions.

This may sound trite and unbelievable, but we have within us the potential to be Christ consciousness now, today. This is not some future event predicted by prognosticators. If we believe that we have to wait for this level of reality, it will never come. If we believe we have to rely on another or for a specific event to occur, it will not happen. In all of these circumstances, we are giving away our power to an external person or event rather than claiming our inherent, divine birthright to be Christ consciousness and live in kingdom consciousness, the core of our very existence. Being born as a human being secures our access to Christ consciousness. Taking each breath gives us the key to open the door to our home in kingdom consciousness. We have to step beyond all that we think we know and surrender to what is; this is the action that will take us across the bridge to our new existence.

The Bridge

Walking across the bridge to the unknown evokes the most basic fear within us. The fight or flight response is triggered, interfering with our ability to walk forward. This deep-seeded fear is manifested by the mind because it does not know what lies on the other side of the bridge. The soul knows exactly what is on the other side; it is home. It is Christ consciousness where the soul can swim in harmony, peace, and love in the sea of oneness. The mind perpetuates the illusion of the separate self. The mind only knows what it perceives through the five physical senses. The soul knows there are more than five senses. It is the *soul senses* that must be awakened for kingdom consciousness to be perceived by the mind.

The simplest soul sense that is known by everyone is intuition. Intuition is the soul speaking to the mind through feelings we often refer to as a gut feeling, hunch, or deep knowingness about the world around us. This clairsentient message from the soul is communicated through a feeling in the body that is then interpreted by the mind. When we receive this message, we sometimes listen to what we are being given. At other times, we discredit the message because there may be no logical or scientific basis for believing that the message should be heeded.

We each have a story, or perhaps many stories, where we did follow our intuition, and this message from our souls directed our actions in what can only be described as the right or highest action. In every moment, there is the potential for unlimited actions. In this range of potential responses, there is a highest or divine choice, an action that supersedes all other choices. The soul message will always be the guidance leading you to the highest and most authentic choice for you. Your soul is the divine spark within you and will always prompt you toward your destiny of returning to kingdom consciousness.

Another flavor of intuition is the ability to hear soul guidance; this is known as clairaudience. This inherent ability allows our divine ears of the mind to actually hear the guidance of the soul. The guidance is perceived as thoughts in the mind— not words spoken out loud, but rather a telepathic ability to hear the voice of the soul. We all have this ability, because telepathic communication is the most natural and elegant form of communication, whether it be soul to human being or between two human beings. Telepathic communication is always available to us; we simply need to open our minds to accept this divine aspect of ourselves and embrace it as an ordinary sense. It allows us to take our first steps across the bridge to kingdom consciousness.

Clairvoyance is another divine ability where we can see what is from a higher vantage point. Each person is given the divine gift of a spiritual eye. Sometimes referred to as the third eye, this spiritual eye is where the soul can share pictures, symbols, colors, and visions with us to guide us on our paths. In Eastern cultures, the third eye is taught to be located on the forehead between the eyebrows. This spiritual eye center opens and allows us another avenue to understand the realm of kingdom consciousness.

Therefore, the soul communicates with us through feeling (clairsentience), telepathic communication (clairaudience), and spiritual seeing (clairvoyance). This triumvirate of divine gifts provides us clear channels to communicate with our souls. These are inherent abilities that, when embraced and integrated into our daily lives, afford us the ability to walk into kingdom consciousness. Jesus used these three gifts in connecting with his soul's guidance, and he encourages us to do the same. These wonderful gifts are only one facet of living in Christ consciousness. What a tremendous way to start our journey over the bridge!

Higher Senses

If we can agree that clairsentience, clairaudience, and clairvoyance are the basic senses required to communicate with our souls, then the next step is to explore higher senses that evolve as we are enveloped in kingdom consciousness. As we walk into kingdom consciousness, we are in a world that cannot be perceived through the five physical senses. The three soul senses of clairsentience, clairaudience, and clairvoyance guide us to the realm of kingdom consciousness. Once we have crossed over the bridge to our natural home, we need higher senses to perceive and cognize the new world we have entered. With the new senses, we will also need new language to be able to describe our interactions in kingdom consciousness.

Jesus taught that our souls are eternal; they exist in a timeless state of grace. Our souls have the divine abilities of omniscience and omnipresence. What are these abilities and how do they manifest in kingdom consciousness? Omniscience is the ability to see all of existence as one interwoven landscape of potential. This layered gradient of multiverses emerges as a natural sense in kingdom consciousness. In a multidimensional universe, we can see the cause and effect of our actions as the energy we conduct moves through physical space. In the multiverse, the energy moves through astral space and cosmic time. In the astral plane of existence, we exist at a higher vibratory level, which transcends the physical plane. On the astral plane, it is our light being, or light body, that exists as an extension of the soul. The higher vibratory nature of the light body allows for the natural navigation of the multiverse. The multiverse, in turn, gives us access to the multitude of potentialities that exist at any given moment. The ability to comprehend the expansiveness of the multiverse and the gradated levels of potentiality is the sense of omniscience.

Omniscience is the higher sense that we use in kingdom consciousness to navigate the matrix of multiversal potential. In every space-time location, or every choice point in the cosmic grid, there are an unlimited number of outcomes for every potential action. When we see the multiversal grid and these potentials, we are using the sense of omniscience. If we break down the word to its essential components, *omni* means one and *science* is the ability to understand or interpret reality.

In this heightened state of awareness, the soul is able to perceive the matrix of potential cosmic choices and outcomes as a multiverse of creation, an infinite cosmic orchestra of divine actions perpetuating the evolution of each soul back to its source of origin, the Godhead. When the soul cognizes the multiverse through the mind, the higher sense of omniscience engages. Once this view of reality is experienced, the splendor of God's magnificence is more clearly understood, and kingdom consciousness is born.

At each choice point in the multiversal matrix, there is the potential for the soul to evolve. For every action, there is an equal and opposite reaction; this is one of the basic laws of Newtonian physics. This law can be applied to choices made by the soul. At each choice point, there are an unlimited amount of infinite actions or choices. The impact of each choice in the matrix will raise the vibratory level of the soul, keep it the same, or reduce the vibratory level of the soul. Actions that are beneficial to the soul's evolution would naturally raise the vibratory level, whereas actions that lower the vibratory level influence the soul's vibration as well. This concept beckons us to think of Lord Buddha's teaching on the eight-fold path. On this path, the concept of right action takes on a new meaning if we understand the vibratory impact of our choices. In the multiverse, there are an infinite number of choices being made that all impact the progressive evolutionary nature of the soul. In kingdom consciousness, the higher senses of the soul allow the consciousness to expand to encapsulate all of these choices. When the soul cognizes this expansive nature, one experiences the higher sense of omniscience.

The alternate higher sense that is experienced in kingdom consciousness is omnipresence. The opening of this sense affords the soul the experience of simultaneously being at all of the soul's choice points in the multiverse. The soul exists as many experiences of itself throughout the matrix. At each choice point, the soul is a spark of God evolving and experiencing itself in an infinite number of ways. The soul is God's expression of itself unfolding and evolving into greater and greater expressions of the infinite and absolute power or energy of God. This constant expansion and evolution allows the beauty of God to be reborn in every moment of eternal expansion. When the soul cognizes the experience of the vast multipresence of God in each choice point of the multiversal matrix, this is the higher sense of omnipresence, a gift from God to each spark of divine energy contributing to the everlasting evolution of infinite expansion.

The bridge to the higher senses is the opening of the soul senses in the mind. This is what Jesus referred to as the gateway to the kingdom of heaven, the key to kingdom consciousness. Each of the higher senses unlocks the potentiality of the mind to elevate to a state of awareness where we can do what Jesus did, and even more. His promise that we can do what he can do is not an idle claim; it is a bold statement of fact predicated on the knowledge that we can in fact live in the kingdom, as Jesus does even to this day.

The Continuation of the Christ Consciousness

I n many of the teachings given to us by Jesus, he tells us repeatedly that he and we will ascend to the kingdom of God and live forever. The attainment of kingdom consciousness is available to everyone. Jesus promised us life eternal, and this eternal life is available in our willingness to step forward into kingdom consciousness.

Every human being has the key to the kingdom. Entry is not based on gender, race, religious belief, social status, or geography. To turn the key in the lock only requires a willingness to suspend current limitations on our greatness and to open our hearts to the vibration of Christ consciousness. As Jesus said, "I am the way, the truth and the life: no man cometh unto the Father, but by me"[1] It is when we allow the vibration of Jesus Christ to permeate our hearts that the higher senses

---

[1] John 14:6. (AV)

emerge, and we turn the key to open the door to the kingdom of God—our destiny as prescribed by Jesus.

The vibration of Christ consciousness has always existed. Throughout history, many sages and saints have opened their hearts to dance in the glory of God's divine love. The vibration enters the spiritual heart and ignites the flame of divine passion, erupting into a relentless pursuit of experiencing the soul engulfed in the love of Christ consciousness. The soul forever seeks the equilibrium of its natural state; this state is the vibration of Christ consciousness.

In the Bible, we are taught that Jesus Christ will come again. In the second coming of Christ, the kingdom of heaven will descend on earth. This divine energy can enter our hearts today, raising our vibrations to the level of Christ consciousness, which is available to all people. When this vibration enters our hearts, we unlock the door to the kingdom of heaven and forever more exist in kingdom consciousness.

The Hum of God's Love

As Christ consciousness enters our hearts, the vibration is sensed as a low-grade, energetic hum throughout the body. The electric current inside of us is permeating all of our cells, igniting within them the memory of our natural state. At first the vibration may feel strange because our physical bodies are not used to perceiving the energetic flow. Over time, however, the hum of God's love moving through our bodies becomes as natural as breathing. In fact, as we first become aware of the vibration, there may be moments when it seems to fade. It is at this juncture that we understand it is possible to maintain this divine vibration. Once we shift our mental perception and physical experience, we open our hearts to invite more waves of Christ consciousness to flow through us.

With the constant flow of Christ consciousness through us, we begin to naturally vibrate at this level of existence. It is this level of vibration that activates our higher senses, allowing the kingdom of God to surround us. Jesus preached that the kingdom of God is within you and around you. He is telling us that the vibration and senses that are activated in this state of consciousness give us the ability to live as Christ lived, breathing in divine grace, performing miracles, teaching others of the beauty of kingdom consciousness, and being a beacon of God's love and light. It is in this spirit that we walk into the kingdom together and live as Jesus Christ lived. As we hum with God's love, let us each acknowledge the existence of Christ consciousness within us and accept an activation of the realm of kingdom consciousness in our lives. Now we can begin to truly live as Christ lived and give as he gave to all people.

Jesus embodied the divine presence of a level of consciousness that allowed the expression of an extraordinary life. In each of us dwells the seeds of this consciousness, the tiny mustard seed that can move mountains. Jesus shared that it is with the faith the size of a mustard seed that when you say *move* to the mountain, it will move. This parable illustrates that we can be that energy that moves the natural order of the world. As we open to embody the divine presence, we become the conduit of the holy energy of God. It is this energy that makes our cells hum and supports our emergence into the kingdom of the Divine.

The miracles that Jesus performed were benchmarks of human performance. They are a road map of human evolution presented to us so that we may pick up the map and follow it to our divine destiny. Jesus did not want to be placed on a pedestal and worshipped as someone greater than ourselves. Jesus wanted us to understand what we are capable of and to step forth into our fullest potential. Jesus did not mingle with kings and queens; he lived with the poor, the disenfranchised, and the outcasts. He did not perceive that he was greater than other people; he was teaching the most ordinary of people just how extraordinary they could be if they followed his teachings.

As a teacher, Jesus shared many stories and parables to illustrate our potential. He was teaching the concepts of right words, rights actions, and right deeds. In the Bible, Jesus is said to have performed miracles. However, were they really miracles, if Jesus said we could do as he did and even more? Were his actions a normal part of human existence that have been suppressed? Did each miracle appear to be an action beyond our human potential simply because our greatness has not yet seen the light of day?

If we use Jesus's words as encouragement and open our souls to the road map he has given us, each one of us can live and thrive in the kingdom consciousness that is our birthright. Let's dip deeper into his words and see if we can glimpse the miraculous in the opening of our true and authentic potential.

The Authentic One

When Jesus walked on earth, he lived in a time of persecution. The Romans lorded over the Holy Lands. The Jewish leaders did not like the disturbance of the young man who was the teacher of the outcasts. As Jesus taught and his words spread, the truth of his message resonated with people; his encouragement of living the truth in a time of oppression was seen as a beacon of light in dark times.

Similarly, we are living in a time of oppression steeped in the darkness of human strife that is perpetuated by an inability to understand that we can live in kingdom consciousness. We are reinforced by constraints that limit our abilities and are governed by the fear of our magnificence. For the most part, these are the mental constructs that we can dissolve through the light of truth. Our truth will ignite the path to our unabridged authenticity, being who we are meant to be.

Authenticity is the emergence of our fullest potential. An authentic person allows the shackles of limitation to be broken and the strength of unbridled potential to be unleashed. The soul has stepped forth as guide and teacher, and the ego has subsided into a supportive role. The blending of soul energy with the energetics of kingdom consciousness gives birth to a truth of personal existence that cannot be denied. It is this forceful emergence that propels the authenticity to arise and catapult the newly born individual into the daily fragrance of Christ consciousness. The perfume of this energetic existence is undeniable. It envelops us as we step boldly into the kingdom of heaven on earth. There is a purity in kingdom consciousness arising from the divine alignment of the cosmic soul and the earthly body. This union of heaven on earth through a human body is the point where the miraculous becomes our everyday existence.

At this time in history, we are lovingly supported by cosmic energies to step forth into the collective kingdom so that all of us may live in this heightened state of awareness. Our bodies have evolved to the point where we can hold the divine vibration in every cell in our bodies. Our minds are opening to a new ability to live as multisensory human beings in a level of consciousness that is beckoning our acceptance. Our souls have descended into our energy fields so fully that they gladly take the wheel as our cosmic chauffeur, driving us forward with effortless ease assured of our destination. The whole of the universe supports our evolution at every level of our existence; there is no more struggle. We are on the edge of a precipice of human potential unprecedented in our lifetime.

With all of the pieces in place, it is up to us to take the key of grace being given to us and place it knowingly into the lock to open the door to the kingdom—our home, destiny, and birthright.

PART III

———⌥———

The Kingdom is already
spread out on the Earth,
and people aren't aware of it.

—Jesus Christ

Our New Life

ow that we have unlocked the door to welcome kingdom consciousness into our lives, what will this mean? Will there be fireworks? Will all of my responsibilities go away? Can I walk away from the daily emotions that saturate my waking hours?

If we turn to Jesus for the answers, he is quite clear about this transition. He teaches us that we can find ourselves in kingdom consciousness in the blink of an eye. With one blink, we have entered the awareness that is our inherent birthright. We have come home to find our true, authentic selves birthed into an awareness of perpetual alignment between our souls' cosmic destiny and the actions of our earthly bodies. This alignment extends to all of our thoughts as well as our emotions. Entrance into the kingdom does not mean the previous version of ourselves is gone; it means that a bolder, stronger, and more self-assured version is born with the grace of God. The divine energetics infiltrating every cell of our bodies aligns with the soul, allowing the birth of our authentic being—the full emergence of who we were born to be with the support of the universe and all of her graces. With support from both heaven and earth, who are we to deny the magnificence of our new existence? It is the birthing of who we were born to be. The comfort of this knowledge supports us as we take our first few steps into life in kingdom consciousness.

As we open our eyes in the new kingdom, it may appear as life as usual. However, we know that life is now anything but usual. In the span of a lifetime, each of us experiences what we believe to be the truth of our existence. The rub is that we were never really seeing our truth; we were only seeing a very small slice of our potential, a constricted energetic reality formed by mass beliefs and held down by delusions of constraint. We are so much bigger, grander, and more magnificent than we were led to believe. In kingdom consciousness, we step out of the cocoon spun by limited beliefs and are born again into an omniscient construct where miracles exceed the limits of our imagination.

A vocabulary for living in kingdom consciousness will need to be built because we are now living in a new reality. In this reality, utilizing our God-given senses allows us to expand beyond previous horizons and walk into a world where the lights are on, exposing the true nature of our existence. We were previously living in a world with blinders on, and once removed, the surging of the light of divine grace opens the third eye to a new level of seeing; we see not only what is in front of us, but more dimensional realities and cosmic shifts in time. The lateral and parallel world of time-bound reality crumbles. We begin to see through a multiversal lens with multisensory perception. Now we are living in kingdom consciousness.

If we transcend the space-time continuum, we emerge into the multiverse of God's grace. We are released from a life constrained in time and limited by space. The ability to perceive existence in a cacophony of orchestrated interconnected combinations pushes us to a new level of not only awareness but of understanding the divine plan. We emerge with the omniscient and omnipresent senses promised to us as Jesus Christ envisioned our potential.

Turning on the soul senses and beginning to use them is similar to exercising a muscle. We need to tap into the new sense and then use it, or exercise it, to make it stronger. It is through the use of our soul senses that alignment occurs with the soul. The soul exists in kingdom consciousness. The mind and body must learn to live in this level of awareness. As the mind and body exercise the multisensory experience, alignment with the soul consumes the flame of the Divine, and the transformation of rebirth occurs.

Jesus revealed that the doorway to the kingdom and God was through Christ consciousness. Christ consciousness envelops the mind and body, allowing the soul to be the cosmic driver. In a state of Christ consciousness, the door to the kingdom does open, and we step into the potential Christ told us we could have while on this earth. In bringing heaven to earth, we each play a critical role as we open the door to the kingdom, walk through, and open our eyes to see the world as though for the first time.

This virgin birth into the realm of Christ consciousness gives each of us the potential to be engaged in the second coming of Christ. Jesus clearly gave us a road map to walk through the door and into the kingdom of God that is within and around us. We must shift our understanding of what the second coming really means and fully embrace our roles in this seismic shift. We are no longer waiting for someone else to make an appearance for the door to God's glory to be opened. We are responsible for opening the door to Christ consciousness, taking the hand of our sisters and brothers, and walking boldly with confidence into kingdom consciousness.

This collective step into a multisensory, multiversal existence is upon us. Saints and sages throughout time have taken the step, and it is now our turn. Our souls are leaping for joy in anticipation of this step. Our minds may sense fear at walking into the unknown. Our bodies may quake with unworthiness, not believing that we can exist in Christ consciousness. Let's embrace the fear and quaking, and transmute them into excitement and anticipation as we collectively take this step into kingdom consciousness.

Jesus explained that the kingdom is entered in the blink of an eye. If you feel afraid, grab the hand of a close friend and blink together. Gather with groups of people who want to blink, and be in the energy of a group. Jesus said, "For where two or three are gathered together in my name, there am I in the midst of them."[1] Christ consciousness exists, so breathe into this level of energetic expansion, commit to blink, and watch the doors to the kingdom open.

---

[1] Matthew 18:20. (AV)

A Collective Blink

As we engage in the practice of blinking into the kingdom, some people will be early adopters, and others will prefer to wait and see what happens to those who go first. This is part of our human nature. Given this dynamic, some people will leap into Christ consciousness while others watch and learn. The early leapers will help to develop a collective vocabulary that can be leveraged to educate the masses who choose not to be in the first wave of adopters. This language will be new but essential to assist with the collective shift of humanity to Christ consciousness.

When we enter kingdom consciousness, our multisensory abilities open allowing us to experience reality through a heightened lens of understanding. Once we stand in the kingdom, we will understand it. It will be the responsibility of the early adopters to communicate the ways of the kingdom to the next wave of people who will choose to blink.

Building a bridge both energetically and supportively will be essential to guiding all of our brothers and sisters to kingdom consciousness. Every one of us has the seeds of Christ consciousness within us. The Jesus seeds exist deep within us, and they are waiting to be activated so that Christ consciousness can be born within each of us. The activation of the seeds is an energetic one that is supported by the love of our divine Father in heaven and the cradled support Mother Earth. We find ourselves living at a moment in time when the energy of the divine floodgates have opened at the same time the resonance of our Mother Earth has risen. The culmination of the heavenly, masculine energy with the feminine, earthly energy results in an energetic field of resonance conducive to the birth of divine children into the kingdom of heaven. This kingdom is here. The energy and support of your cosmic father and earthly mother hold you in a cocoon of safety so you can push open the door and live forevermore in the kingdom of heaven.

Are you ready to blink?

The Bridge Builders

I n the course of evolution, the fervent few who take the first steps outside of what is collectively agreed upon as reality will be ostracized. "How dare you step beyond the boundaries of what we find normal and comfortable to upset the status quo! How is it possible that *this way* is not the *only way?* Why are we upsetting the proverbial apple cart to make applesauce when we were just fine with the apples?"

In times of great change, great leaders are called. At the time of the calling, the leaders are not great; they are ordinary people who are plucked from the daydream of everyday reality, and through the fire of transformation, are reborn as a warrior. The forces against social change become so great that the ones who are called combust in the flame of social rejection, only to rise like a phoenix from the ashes of their former selves into a newly born version of their potential. This new human being is strong beyond strength, wise beyond wisdom, and committed beyond all commitment to lead the social change required to pull humanity to the next level of reality.

These warriors of our time will be called the bridge builders. They are not destined to build a physical bridge over a body of water, but rather they will build a bridge from our current level of awareness to kingdom consciousness. By taking our hands, they will gently lead us to a life engulfed in Christ consciousness. The bridge builders will develop a new language to shift our consciousness; while at the same time they are firmly anchored in the new reality. By standing on one side of the bridge with extended arms, we who are just opening our eyes can be guided step by step across the river of doubt to the safety of our higher potential. These steps will initiate a seismic shift in our worldview and rattle our bones to the core.

In the gospel of Thomas, Jesus predicted that once you discover the truth, you will be deeply disturbed, and ultimately amazed. When we begin to see the world through the eyes of God, we will be disturbed. The shackles of restraint will dissolve, leaving us free to live a life beyond what we can even begin to imagine today. The disturbance emerges from the dissolution of our current worldview as it slips into the past, allowing for the birth of our expanded and evolved existence. The amazement arises from seeing reality from an omniscient perspective. The opening of new senses coupled with an understanding of our full potential culminates into a golden key that unlocks the door to kingdom consciousness.

As the key turns in the lock, the click activates within us the dormant DNA that has been waiting for this moment. Science has told us that we only use a small portion of our brains, and that we have DNA that does not appear to have a purpose. Do you believe that God would have architected us to have parts that simply have no purpose? Or does it make more sense to imagine that we have been equipped with everything that we need to take this step into Christ consciousness, to understand that we already have the ability to live in kingdom consciousness and only need to step forward to claim our divine inheritance? It is our birthright to live a divine life. It is our destiny to live in kingdom consciousness. It is our natural evolutionary path to allow the full potential of the physical body and mind to merge with our soul as our Christed nature is born. Christ consciousness is nothing more than the ability to embrace our fullest potential as we emerge onto a new plane of existence. It is nothing less than our commitment to use every God-given gift to propel ourselves forth into birthing the kingdom of God on earth.

When we speak of the second coming of Christ and living in the kingdom of God, did you really believe that you would not play a significant role in this event? Did you think that God expected you to stand on the sidelines while his kingdom was birthed? Did you imagine that someone else would do all of the work as we stood idly by watching the creation of the greatest moment in human history?

Jesus teaches us over and over that we will be the ones to do great works. We are the ones who hold the spark of the Divine within our hearts. We are destined to participate in the birthing of heaven on earth. We are the ones we have been waiting for; the ones to breathe Christ consciousness into reality and build God's kingdom on earth.

Knowing this truth, it is time for you to step forth to assist in the evolutionary leap of mankind. You know in every fiber

The Leap

In a matter of seconds, a shift to kingdom consciousness is made. The rapidity of the shift fails to compare to the significance of the event. The ability to break through to a level of sustainable consciousness that encompasses Christ consciousness is amazing. Some may call it a miracle. I call it evolution.

As a species, evolution is the key to survival. In these troubled times, an evolutionary leap is required to lift us beyond our current scarcity mentality to a plane of existence where abundance reigns. Illness and aging are time-bound consequences that can be shifted to health and vitality with the leap into Christ consciousness. Jesus healed the sick and raised the dead by lifting the consciousness of his brothers and sisters to his level of consciousness, thus eliminating the need for the body to stay trapped in lower dimensional consciousness. Each of us has the ability to walk forth into Christ consciousness; to get there, we must make an active and conscious commitment to breathe in God's glory with each breath. Being centered in God's grace embellishes our vibrational capacity to live in his kingdom in every moment. This is not a someday wish or a tomorrow occurrence. The activation of our Christ consciousness exists today. Jesus assured us the kingdom of heaven is within us; it is not in some distant land or far away in the sky. The kingdom exists for us to enter the very moment we accept our magnificence and acknowledge our birthright to be as Christ was, to be in Christ consciousness and live in God's kingdom.

The leap may seem too great for us. We may be afraid of what stepping into our greatness means for us and for those we love. We may hesitate because the unknown is scary, and we do not want to go first. Jesus Christ went first for all of us. He was the way-shower, teacher, and guide to what each of us can be if we simply take the leap of faith to kingdom consciousness.

As the disciple Paul said, "Faith is the substance of things hoped for, the evidence of things not seen."[1] Faith is what propels us forth when we have doubt or fear. Faith that Jesus Christ was born on this earth to give us a road map to our greatness resonates deeply within our souls. Allow this vibration of certainty to rise in your awareness, and feel the comfort that walking in Jesus's steps to the kingdom will bring to your soul.

The calling we have to enter into kingdom consciousness is within us from the moment we take our first breath. The yearning to exist in a heightened level of awareness pulls the soul towards our true destiny. The steps are right in front of us; Jesus showed us the way. Believe in your greatness, take the

---

[1] Hebrews 11:1. (AV)

steps, and then a running leap into kingdom consciousness. There is a bridge that has been built from where we are to where we are going. Saints and mystics have walked this path for centuries. Our momentum as a collective consciousness has been accelerated. We can each leap for the kingdom, knowing in full faith the bridge to our magnificence has been paved with the steps of our ancestors.

Will you take my hand and leap?

Are You Ready?

I t is said that if you take one step toward the Divine, the Divine will take a thousand steps towards you. With each acknowledged step towards kingdom consciousness, the kingdom is racing towards you. Given this dynamic, it makes sense that a single leap by you will propel you into Christ consciousness as your awareness is engulfed in higher vibrational consciousness.

The key to the leap is to ask yourself this fundamental question. *Are you ready?* Are you ready to accept a life engulfed in Christ consciousness? Are you ready to leap into kingdom consciousness? Are you ready to step into your full potential and breathe in the waves of divine grace? Are you ready?

In all religions and belief systems, there is always a pivotal point in the human experience when the grace of God descends and the human soul ascends, to meet in the birth of a new life anointed with a vibratory explosion of higher awareness, bringing the newly birthed child to the doorstep of the kingdom.

Jesus said, "Whoever among you becomes like an infant will know the Kingdom."[1] The entrants to the kingdom are as small children because they have been reborn into a new level of awareness, a consciousness more expansive and fuller in ability to perceive the greatness of kingdom consciousness. It is the shift in perception and expansion of the senses that opens the door to the kingdom.

The ability to be reborn into Christ consciousness resides in every one of us; no one is excluded. This inclusive manifestation of Christ consciousness, while we breathe the air of our earth, beckons to each of us. We are called to greatness through the gentle tugging of our souls. She knows the path to the kingdom and has read the road map that Jesus gave us. She wants to take your hand and walk with you into your highest potential.

You must speak the words of your commitment to walk into Christ consciousness out loud: "Yes, I am ready." Your voice will reverberate through heaven and earth with your willingness to be engulfed in Christ consciousness. "Yes, I am ready." With your energy and intention focused on taking your leap of faith into kingdom consciousness, again say it out loud. "Yes, I am ready."

With the words, "Yes, I am ready," you have taken your step toward Christ consciousness. Allow Christ consciousness to take one thousand steps towards you. As you open your new eyes as a Christed being, watch as the kingdom emerges into your presence.

---

[1] Davies, *The Gospel of Thomas*, p, 61.

What Are the Signs?

As you take the leap and become immersed in Christ consciousness, what are the changes you will experience? As we abide in Christ consciousness, our lives become a living representation of all things possible. There is nothing that is not possible. In this inspired and limitless level of awareness, we create our reality in every moment; this is a powerful shift from our former beliefs of limitation, lack, and scarcity. Now we have shifted into a consciousness with the characteristics of unbounded, fully engaged creativity to manifest a world of perpetual unlimited potential. This is the sense of omniscience, the ability to see all and know all, because we are creating each moment. We are creating our reality at the level of Christ consciousness. It unfurls with a distinctive imprint of divine architecture.

In the state of Christ consciousness, the idea of "everything is connected" takes on a whole new meaning. Everything seen and unseen is connected at the most basic vibratory level.

The singing of the atoms and subparticles that comprise all physical matter harmonize with unseen, non-physical matter to create a web of interconnectivity that can be cognized through our omniscient senses. In Vedic philosophy, this is known as Indra's web. In quantum physics, this interconnectivity is explained through string theory. In the Bible, the omniscient awareness of our reality is exemplified in Jesus as he performed miracles. Jesus could see the world through omniscient eyes. His miracles were the alignment of the interconnected nature of all of existence. The ability to heal the sick, cure the lame, and raise the dead emanate from an internal alignment with the vibration of the divine presence. Also known as the Holy Spirit or Holy Ghost, this vibration lifts the energetic nature of everything it touches, thus shifting whatever is touched into alignment with the highest vibratory levels. This alignment spontaneously creates the highest level of divine vibration, resulting in what we may label as miracles; in reality they are an energetic alignment.

As we enter into kingdom consciousness and vibrate at the level of Christ consciousness, we can also perform energetic alignments. When we speak of Jesus, we typically say he performed miracles. What if we change our language, and instead of a performance, we refer to his actions as an *alignment?* He aligned the energetic vibratory nature of people, and in that alignment, people became healthy, vital, and whole, no matter the previous state of their existence.

As we live in Christ consciousness, we are also fully capable of aligning our vibratory levels, and the vibratory levels of everyone around us, to maintain our daily existence in the kingdom. The hum of our divine nature penetrates every aspect of our lives. The vibration is not only in us but is also found all around us. This vibratory level of Christ consciousness allows our ability to live in health and abundance, while also raising the level of vibration around us. In this space, we find that we attract to us the elements to continue our existence at this level. All that we need to sustain and perpetuate our Christ consciousness will be made manifest. In this state of existence, the universal order of divine nature architects the expansion of our energy to support the entire cosmos. In return for our commitment to sustain this level of Christ consciousness, the doors of the kingdom open, and all that we require to continue our expansion is provided.

Jesus knew that as we came to accept the magnificence of our vibratory nature, we would naturally use the gifts from this level of consciousness to raise others to the same or higher level. He knew that when we committed to living in kingdom consciousness, all of our needs would be met. He knew that once we began to live our lives at this level of fullest potential, we would continue to evolve and achieve even greater heights than he did.

Knowing this, a sense of urgency arises in our hearts as we realize the magnitude of our collective shift. If we are ready to step fully into Christ consciousness, we can actively work with our brothers and sisters to align their vibratory nature to ours and, in doing so, open them to a world of kingdom consciousness. Jesus taught that we are our brothers' keeper. We are all here to inherit our divine birthright to Christ consciousness and then raise our brothers and sisters to vibrate at the same level.

This collective shift for all people can also be known as our ascension. It is an ascension of all human beings to higher

Walk in His Steps

Jesus came to show us what was possible, and what is possible. He embraced his divine nature and, through teaching, was able to give a vibratory shift to the people he touched with his words. Over two thousand years later, his words still bring alignment of our hearts and souls in the sayings and parables of his truth. It is taught that it is only through the truth of his way that we will reach God realization. He is telling us that it is only through the attainment of Christ consciousness that we can enter God's kingdom and intimately know this force that transcribes the world into a higher diction of divine enactment.

It is through our passage into Christ consciousness that our own divine nature emerges in this plane of physical reality. We are the link between the God consciousness of heaven and the physical reality of earth. As the midpoint between heaven and earth, it is our responsibility to open our hearts and allow the soul space for the Divine to flood our beings with the divine spark, to allow the wind of celestial compassion to fan the flame of the divine spark, igniting within us the birth of Christ consciousness.

The vibration of Christ consciousness arises within us and then flows out of us to touch everything we encounter. Every person, plant, and animal is touched by Christ consciousness radiating from our bodies. This vibration is continually shifting and lifting so that all of life is elevated to a higher vibration. Jesus said, "I am the light of the world."[1] The light is the light of God, the vibration of God that leads to the unlimited potential of creation by mankind while living on the earth.

I AM is the divine vibratory signature of God. I AM is the vibratory essence of Jesus Christ. I AM is the birthright of each human being, opening the doors to the kingdom of the Divine.

As you walk in Jesus's steps to claim your vibratory birthright, say I AM.

> I AM God's light.
> I AM God's love.
> I AM Christ's love on earth.

You are the vessel through which Christ's vibration touches the world. Saint Teresa of Avila, a 16th century Carmelite nun and Spanish mystic, reminds us that we are the hands, feet, and eyes of Christ in her prayer "Christ Has No Body".

---

[1] John 8:12. (AV)

Christ has no body but yours,
No hands, no feet on Earth but yours,
Yours are the eyes with which he looks
compassion on this world,
Yours are the feet with which he walks to do
good,
Yours are the hands, with which he blesses all
the world.
Yours are the hands, yours are the feet,
Yours are the eyes, you are his body.
Christ has no body now but yours,
No hands, no feet on Earth but yours,
Yours are the eyes with which he looks
compassion on this world.
Christ has no body now on Earth but yours.

You are the embodiment of Christ consciousness. You are the living Christ on earth. You are the hands that do Christ's work. Your eyes are the eyes of God looking with love and compassion at his creation.

As you accept this divine inheritance and become the vessel for Christ consciousness, you automatically receive the key to the kingdom. Kingdom consciousness is revealed when Christ consciousness is embodied. Walk boldly into kingdom consciousness so that we may collectively birth the kingdom of heaven on earth. There is no waiting for the second coming of Jesus Christ—we *are* the second coming of the birth of Christ consciousness on this earth. We are the bodies that will hold this vibrational energy. We are the ones for which we have been waiting.

As we each acknowledge this birthright, our collective shift to higher levels of consciousness will proceed unimpeded. Through the collective union of our Christed energies, we will give birth to the kingdom of God on earth and open the doors to the golden age of peace. In the Bible, it is said that after the second coming of Christ, peace will reign for one thousand years.

Let's all agree that we can open the door to the millennium of peace. As we embody Christ consciousness and give birth to the kingdom of heaven on earth, kingdom consciousness will spread like wildfire. In the blink of an eye, we can catapult ourselves to the next level of our evolution. It is time to activate our dormant DNA and light up all areas of our brains to expand our God-given senses to experience what life can truly be. All things are possible; we are only limited by our current understanding of reality. Dare to take the step to embrace Christ consciousness. Be courageous enough to push open the doors to the kingdom. Be loving and compassionate as you hold the hands of your brothers and sisters, so that we can collectively walk forth into a destiny that beckons to each one of us.

In the blink of an eye, we become Christ consciousness. With the turn of the key, we open the door to kingdom consciousness. In the split second of your commitment to birthing the kingdom of heaven on earth, your destiny and ability to do things even greater than Jesus is born.

Welcome to our new kingdom. Let's take it one step at a time.

Giving blessings, strength, and courage to each soul who embarks on this journey:

> May God's grace envelop you,
> Jesus' love embrace you, and
> the gifts of the Holy Spirit
> be born with each breath.

God is waiting for us. I AM ready.

Appendix: Soul Journaling

The practice of soul journaling is one that I have engaged in for many years. The inspiration for this simple, daily dance with my soul came forth with a clarity that compelled me to integrate it into my daily morning ritual, an immersion into that sacred time set aside for me. Your soul has the road map for your life; she wants to guide you to your destiny with grace and ease. I would like to share this personal practice with you in the hope that it will forever change your life as it has changed mine.

Soul guidance is the key to unlocking the magnificence of your life. There are many ways to connect to this personalized guidance. Whatever way you choose to use, it is important to know that connecting to it is like using a muscle: the more you use it, the stronger the connection will become. My process involves the following steps that have worked for me in my quest for continued personal evolution.

For me, the best time to engage in my soul journaling is in the morning, when I wake up. In the quiet of my sacred morning space, I begin with several minutes of deep breathing to center myself in the present moment. With each deep breath in, I feel the glory of God's grace entering me and inspiring every cell in my body to be open to receive. With each exhalation, I feel God's love as it flows into the world around me. I continue my deep breathing until I feel my muscles relax and the peace of God's breath in my mind.

In this heightened state of awareness, I begin to listen. I listen with what I call my divine ears, the ears that tune into the subtle vibrations that the soul emits to provide us with messages for our personal journey. In this silent space, I begin to hear words from my soul. These are not words that I hear externally like a person speaking to me, but rather words that are gently birthed internally in my mind. It may be one word, or perhaps a sentence. Sometimes I have the experience of many sentences being strung together, providing me exactly what I need to know at that time in my life. As I begin to hear the words in my mind with my divine ears, I write the words in my soul journal. During this process, I relax into the words, allowing them to wash over me as I capture their essence on the page. I do not worry about spelling, grammar, or punctuation; rather, I simply allow the words to flow and write them in my journal as they are presented to me.

It is at this point in the process that I sometimes find that my ego will attempt to interfere with the process. The ego begins to judge what is being written in my journal and even criticizes the entire process. To overcome this interjection of the ego into my soul journaling, I have developed a process that will allow me to continue to integrate my soul guidance while rejecting the noise of the ego. Once I have written the sacred words from my soul, I put my soul journal away and do not read it until the following morning. I find that this pause between the reception of my soul words and reading the soul guidance gives me time to push my ego out of the way; this allows space for the guidance to be presented to me as it was intended: without judgment or criticism, but rather with the warmth, love, and evolutionary impulse in which the words were birthed.

Using this cycle of receiving the soul words and then waiting a day before reading my soul guidance, I wake up each morning and read the soul guidance from the previous day with an indescribable joy in my heart. The soul words provide me with an intimate gift each morning, a bounty of sacred insight into my personal evolution that propels me forth with the full faith that my soul is guiding each step that I take on my journey. This gift has fueled my growth over many years; it has become such an integral part of my personal evolution that waking up each morning without the words of my soul journaling would be like waking up without the sun rising. It is an essential part of my authentic essence. My existence is predicated on this daily sacred exchange with my soul. Her loving hand guides my day, and I can feel the grace and ease as it unfolds in each moment.

The process of soul journaling then becomes a repetitive daily ritual. You wake up and read the soul guidance from the previous day, breathe into that silent nurturing space, and receive more soul guidance that is set aside and read the next morning. This cycle of receiving from your soul and then giving of your full, authentic self to the world becomes a sacred act

In Gratitude and Appreciation

It is with deep gratitude and sincere appreciation that I thank the following people:

To my parents, Robert and Maryann: for your unconditional love and support throughout my journey.

To my brother and his family, Bob, Vicky, Stacie, Diana, and Richard: for love perpetuated in every breath.

To the Clark Tri-Pod, Kimberly, Michael, and Kai: for making me a part of your family and loving me in all ways.

To Panache and Jan Desai: for love and support with no boundaries.

To my continually expanding soul family, Anne, Michael, Robert, Mary Beth, Lee, Deborah, Peter, Lori, Camryn, Chrissa, Sebastian, Chuck, Peggy, Gertie, Bernadette, Mary, Karla, Ken, Tracey, Cheryl, and Lucas: for loving me without reservation and for the joy found in reuniting again.

About the Author

Laurel Geise is an inspirational teacher, author, and speaker who empowers people around the world to live an authentic, soul-guided life. When the practicality of real-world examples combine with the awakened energy of her message, the evolutionary impulse ignited by Laurel's teachings will lift and shift your consciousness. Once experienced, you will step beyond what you can imagine to redefine the future of your life.

Laurel's background is a unique combination of thirty years as a business executive coupled with decades of seeking personal growth insights from world religions and belief systems. Blending together undergraduate studies in psychology and information technology, graduate studies in business, and doctoral studies in spirituality, she enthusiastically weaves a vision of unbounded human potential that is calling to be unleashed. She is an ordained interfaith minister and lives in Florida.

Additional books by Laurel include *The Book of Life: Universal Truths for a New Millennium*, *The New Laws of Spirit*, and *Prophetic Leadership: A Call to Action*. They are available from www.amazon.com and www.bn.com.

To ignite *your* soul guided life, visit www.laurelgeise.com.